NONE
SHALL BE
BARREN

NONE
SHALL BE
BARREN

Michal As A Case Study

David Sadiq

Royalpriestofjesus

authorHOUSE®

AuthorHouse™
1663 Liberty Drive
Bloomington, IN 47403
www.authorhouse.com
Phone: 1-800-839-8640

First published by AuthorHouse   11/23/2011

ISBN: 978-1-4678-7805-0 (sc)
ISBN: 978-1-4678-7806-7 (hc)
ISBN: 978-1-4678-7807-4 (ebk)

Printed in the United States of America

Any people depicted in stock imagery provided by Thinkstock are models, and such images are being used for illustrative purposes only.
Certain stock imagery © Thinkstock.

Dedication

This book is dedicated to the glory of God for His Holy Spirit upon man and to all families worldwide who are facing the challenges of having the fruits of the womb. I want to assure you that God's covenant of fruitfulness will visit you as you read this book.

Acknowledgement

The joy and pleasures I have in completing this book will not be completed without appreciating the people who have contributed immensely their time, patience, prayers, support and expertise to seeing it done better.

My first thank goes to the Almighty God who by His Holy Spirit inspired me to start and complete this book. He is my source of inspiration, to Him alone belongs wisdom, glory, honour, power, dominion and majesty, for ever and ever, amen.

I am most grateful to my wife Mrs Victoria Sadiq, for her writing the preface.

I want to thank my tutors, Reverend Dr. Gideon Bakare and Dr. Emmanuel Tukasi for their constructive criticisms which encouraged and led to re-writing of many things in this book.

I specially want to thank pastor Dele Macaulay of the RCCG House of Liberty London, written the foreword of this book.

I am particularly grateful to my Pastor, Festus Wanogho for his assistance and encouragement. I want to say thank you to Busola Erinfolami, Fehintoluwa Onadola Olunowo, for their support.

Finally, I wish to express my sincere thanks to Pastor Williams Oluleye and all the members of CGRM International, Lagos, Nigeria. I want to say thank you to all the members of RCCG Winners Assembly parish London. The good Lord blesses you all. Amen.

Foreword

Barrenness has brought despondency, sorrow, regret, guilt, shame and separation to many homes.

The author of this book makes it clear that God never changed His plan concerning the promise He gave to man right from the beginning of creation to be fruitful and multiply.

Then at this juncture, we pause and ask the question. Who is actually responsible for barrenness? Is it the devil, man or God?

This book has uncovered the hidden treasure and shed more light on how families can be blessed with the fruits of the womb.

I have no doubt that as you read this book and key into the promises of God concerning fruitfulness. The Blessings of the fruits of the womb will surely be your portion in the name of Jesus Christ.

Just as it was in the times of old that neighbours, families and friends rejoiced with Abraham and Sarah, Elkanah and Hannah, Zacharias and Elizabeth they will surely rejoice with you too as it is written "You shall be blessed above all peoples, there shall not be a male or female barren among you or among your livestock"—Deuteronomy 7:14.

Dele Macaulay
Parish Pastor RCCG House of Liberty

Preface

It is the desire of every married woman to have children for her husband. Children she can love and care for. Children she can call her own. Children she can nurture and watch grow up into fine men and women. Therefore, when a married woman is unable to conceive and give birth to children after many attempts there is fear of that marriage not lasting for a long time even when it does, the joy that is meant to be between the husband and the wife might probably be gone!

When we look at the promises of God in the Bible for mankind, one outstanding promise is that we should be fruitful and multiply, Genesis chapter 1 verse 28. It is this promise of God to us that my husband is bringing to light in this book, to give hope to many families who have been trying to have children without success and to those who think that they do not have a chance to conceive because of their past misdeeds. One important thing I will like to point out here is that God forgives and wipes away every sin that is confessed sincerely and from a truly repentant heart.

When I could not conceive immediately after our wedding, I began to fret and became worried. My husband on the other hand was calm. As far as he was concerned, God had not said that we are barren. My husband had God's promises, he knew what God's word says and he taught me to hold on to these promises and today we have two beautiful girls.

In this book my husband looks at the assertion that people make about Michal being barren even though the bible says she had no child. My husband through the inspiration and help of the Holy Spirit comes to conclude that Michal was not barren and therefore is every daughter of Abraham. Every child of God already has God's promises for his or her life written in the Bible, all that is needed is to read and claim them by faith. I sincerely pray that as you read this book you will clearly understand that God intends for you to have children of your own. As you hold on to these promises you will experience the joy of parenthood.

MRS VICTRORIA SADIQ

Table Of Contents

Introduction

"Sarah, Rebecca, Rachel, Hannah, Elizabeth

Just to name a few . . .

There are many stories of women in the Bible who struggle with infertility and the pain of not having children.

The Bible not only shares the stories of these "barren women" but also offers hope and comfort during these times.

God indeed is the creator of life and the God of comfort and peace." By Juniper Berry.

"For this cause the Lord will be waiting, so that he may be kind to you; and he will be lifted up, so that he may have mercy on you; for the Lord is a God of righteousness: there is a blessing on all whose hope is in him. O people, living in Zion, at Jerusalem, your weeping will be ended; he will certainly have mercy on you at the sound of your cry; when it comes to his ear, he will give you an answer." Isaiah 30:18-19 (BBE)

Most often I have heard teachers and preachers of Gospel teaching and preaching that the only woman that God "allowed" to be barren in the Bible was Michal the daughter of Saul, the wife of King David. How very untrue is this!

God's covenant with man is to be "fruitful, multiply and replenish the earth." He is a covenant keeping God and not a man to lie; there is no man or woman that was born to be barren according to the promise of God.

Some might be asking "what happens to those that have been confirmed medically that they could not bear children?" In this book, I want to explain to both Christians and non-Christians audience that Barrenness does not come from God. If we have to agree that medically some have been written off as never to conceive, this can only be caused by man/woman themselves.

Take for instance a man that smoke and drinks heavily according to medical believe is unhealthy habit which leads to vasoconstriction that reduce the size of the vein thereby reducing the amount of blood reaching the vital organs. If such man could not impregnate his wife and (he) remain childless, could we blame his 'barrenness' on God?

Excessive use of hot bath tubs or exposure to too much heat has been associated with barrenness. Too much exposure to heat in the groin area can affect the quality of sperm.

Occupation is another hazard that could lead to male sterility. There are some particular jobs that could expose a man to some harmful chemical or poisons inhalations which could wreak havoc on a man's fertility.

In women, scarring of the uterus as a result of sexually transmitted disease or endometriosis is a major cause of barrenness. Poor nutrition, ovarian cysts, pelvic infection, tumours, multiple sex partners, are among other factors in women that leads to barrenness which are not from God but man inflicted due to environmental pollution and poor personal hygiene.

It is in the nature of man to find someone to blame for their own mistakes and errors Gen. 3:9-13, thus a man that has been smoking all his life despite warning from the doctors that smoking is dangerous to their health or a woman who does not take personal hygiene important or those who have multiple partners and contract STD might want to blame God for their inability to become parent.

The good news is that it does not matter what your case is, as God clearly stated that " . . . I will have mercy on whom I will have mercy, and I will have compassion on whom I will have compassion." Romans 9:15. Pray to this God of Mercy who is Compassionate about you as you begins to read this book, have faith in Him and He will re-write your story. I decree by the Authority in the Name of Jesus that as you are reading this book, you will have a divine visitation as God visited Sara. Amen.

Chapter One

In The Begining

Genesis 1:27-28

> *27. So God created man in His own image, in the image of God created He him; male and female crated he them.*
>
> *28. And God bless them and God said unto them, Be fruitful, and multiply, and replenish the earth, and subdue it; and have dominion over the fish of the sea, and over the fowl of the air, and over every living thing that moved upon the earth.*

In the beginning God crated man and woman to be *fruitful, multiply, replenish the earth, subdue and have dominion.* Initially before man was formed, God as a master craftsman first created animals and the beast which are going to be useful for man.

Genesis 1:24

> **And God said, let the earth bring forth the living creature after his kind, cattle, and creeping things and beast of the earth after his kind and it was so.**

Something that is worthy of notice in the above scripture is that God not only created cattle, but after their own kind i.e. male and female cattle were created. This was the same truth about every *"creeping things and beast, whales, and every winged fowl."*

The important question we need to ask here is why did God created these beasts after their kinds.

Genesis 1:20-22

20. And God said, Let the waters bring forth abundantly the moving creature that hath life, and fowl that may fly above in the open firmament of heaven.

21. and God created great whales, and every living creature that moved, which the waters brought forth abundantly, after their kind, and every winged fowl after his kind: and God saw that it was good.

22 And God blessed them, *saying, be fruitful, and multiply, and fill the waters in the seas, and let fowl multiply the earth.*

From the above scripture, it was the same commandment that God gave to man to be "fruitful, multiply and fill and replenish the earth" that He gave unto the whales the beast and the winged fowls, but first God created the beast, whales, winged fowls after their own kinds (male and female) for the purpose of procreation. But alas man was alone!

After God has finished the creation of the beast and the whales, the winged fowls after their own kind and pronounced them blessed, God realised that before man could fulfil the commandment of been fruitful, multiply and replenishment of the earth man has to produce his own kind too. But because man (unlike the beast, whales, and the winged fowls) is a unique creature, God's own 'kind' who was made out of him. Man as a direct image of God.

Genesis 2:18-22

18. And the Lord God said, it is not good that the man should be alone; I will make him an help meet for him.

21. And the Lord God caused a deep sleep to fall upon Adam, and he slept: and he took one of his ribs and closed up the flesh instead thereof;

22. And the rib, which the Lord God had taken from man, made he a woman, and brought her unto the man.

The woman was made out of man not only to be an "helpmeet" for him (Gen.2:18) but at the same time to be the channel by which the commandment of been "fruitful, multiply and replenish" the earth will be fulfilled.

It is not by accident or coincidence that you are married to that man/or woman. You are been brought together to fulfil one of the greatest commandment of God, to be fruitful and replenish the earth. It is a rare privilege which was not given to other creatures but man as heir to the Almighty God Himself.

Chapter Two

Be Fruitful And Multiply

"Behold, children are a heritage of Yahweh.
The fruit of the womb is his reward.
As arrows in the hand of a mighty man,
So are the children of youth.
Happy is the man who has his quiver full of them.
They won't be disappointed when they speak with their
enemies in the gate." Psalms 127:3-5. [BBE]

"I would therefore have the younger women marry, bear children, rule in domestic matters, and furnish the Adversary with no excuse for slander." 1 Timothy 5:14 [WEYMOUTH]

Man was created to be perfect as God Himself is perfect (Deut. 32:4). God created the universe, the heavenly, the galaxy, the angelic beings etc. God in a way had looked at himself as been fruitful, in essence been successful and he created man to do same.

To be fruitful means producing many good results; profitable or successful. According to John Tay in his book God's Destiny for You, he explained that one of the evidences of divine visitation upon our lives is fruitfulness. In the parable of the sower, our Lord

Jesus spoke about the seed that fell on good ground and produced a harvest of thirtyfold, sixtyfold, and a hundredfold. (Mark 4:1-9).[1] God in His omnipotent majesty looked at His work of creations and concluded that He is successful for the bible says:

> **"And God saw everything that he had made, and behold, it was very good . . . ." Genesis 1:31**.

This was a statement of a successful master planner, master builder Himself upon seen His handwork, He cannot help but exclaimed " . . . behold, it was very good". Man was created for the same purpose of mastery in creation and fruitfulness.

WHAT IS MULTIPLICATION?

Before man was formed, God has created the Angelic beings that ministered to Him in the heavenly (Revelation 5:11, 12). Angel is from the Greek word 'Angelo's' (ang-el-oss), Strong's N32: [From *angello*, "to deliver a message"] which means a messenger. Angels are mere servants or messenger, heavenly personage attendant upon God who He sends on errands for one assignment or the other. (Exodus 23:20; Dan. 6:22; Luke 1:26.)

As every successful businessman (remember we said earlier that God is a successful master builder. Gen.1:31) will want to have a heir or progeny that will continue to run his vast empire of business, as no man will want to entrust his business into the hands of a 'mere servants' or messengers. God also decided to have an heir, progeny, someone that looks like Him, carry His traits, gene and chromosomes that will represent Him on the earth to continue the perfection of His work of creation.

Genesis 1:27

27. So God created man in His own IMAGE, in the IMAGE (His likeness) of God created he him . . .

Not only did God created man in His own replica, the bible says;

"And the Lord God formed man of the dust of the ground, and BREATHED, into his nostrils the BREATH OF LIFE; and man became a living soul." Genesis 2:7.

The very moment God breathe the breath of life into man's nostril, man become like God having all of God's traits and characteristics. From that moment, man enters into the commandment of fruitful and multiplication, to produce offspring after their kinds, children that will continue to bear resemblance of the most High God.

Procreation was part of Adam and Eve's purpose as seen throughout the Old Testament where children were seen as blessings and a heritage from Jehovah. But unfortunately, man was deceived and fell. (Genesis 3:1-24).

The purpose of God for bringing a man and woman together as husband and wife beside companionship is to have godly and healthy children to fill the earth. Are there any habits or behaviour in your house that does not glorify the name of God? This is time to repent and confess them so that the promise of God will be fulfil in your home.

Chapter Three

The Fall Of Man In The Garden Of Eden

"I've learned a lot about women. I think I've learned exactly how the fall of man occurred in the Garden of Eden. Adam and Eve were in the Garden of Eden, and Adam said one day, Wow, Eve, here we are, at one with nature, at one with God, we'll never age, we'll never die, and all our dreams come true the instant that we have them. And Eve said, Yeah ... it's just not enough is it?" Bill Hicks

"Be sober and self-controlled. Be watchful. Your adversary the devil walks around like a roaring lion, seeking whom he may devour." 1 Peter 5:8. [WEB]

All the green plants were given to man (Adam) and his partner (Eve) for food except the tree of the knowledge of good and evil. The tree was to be so abhorred that a death warning was given if the fruit on the tree was to be eaten (Genesis 2:17). The question is why would God, if He cares so much about man and never want him to die put a 'lethal and poisonous' tree in the midst of the garden where man lives?

God created man in His own image, to have all His attributes, characters, dominion and freewill.

According to Boulay . . . The God of Old Testament has many human attributes-he is jealous; and vindictive . . . [2]

Man was created to be a free moral agent capable of making and executing decisions on his own. Another reason why the tree must have been put in the Garden is to serve as an acid test to man from His Creator whether he will obey Him fully and possibly for man to learn to trust God. We should understand that God had earlier (before man was created) suffered betrayal from one of His creature Satan who rebelled against Him.

Henry Morris in his book stated that man was not created as automation, but as a free being with the moral ability to love God or reject God as he should choose. There was not the slightest reasons why he should sin, but he could if he so desired. [3]

Genesis chapter 3 was introduce with serpent been more subtle; the question here again is, why serpent, who is the serpent and why does he have to tempt the woman? The serpent was one of the beast that God created earlier for man to have a friendly dominion. Could it be that this serpent has been influenced by an 'external' force that was not mentioned?

Dixon in his book observed that from where did this talking serpent come? The beasts of the field had not been able to talk in any of the creation narrative. The narrative provides us with a great mystery, and within an underlying clue. This was no ordinary serpent. The phrase, ' . . . was more subtle than any beast of the field,' is better understood when read in a partitive sense. That is, this serpent is set apart from all beasts, meaning he is part of the kingdom, but is not necessarily from that kingdom. The text could be understood as ' . . . subtle as no other of the beasts . . .' The eerie presence rocks us. The serpent has been there in the animal kingdom, but some other being is present of which the reader has not been informed . . . [4]

Could this 'other being' be the same Satan I mentioned earlier who betrayed God and possibly want man to do same? Wenham stated that early Jewish and Christian commentators identified the snake with Satan or devil . . . [5]

Satan used the serpent that was more subtle, clever with dazzling colours to deceive the woman (Eve) who was so naive to carry out his plan of deceptions. The same way the devil today uses subtlety and dazzling things to deceive men. I want to believe in his cunning way, the serpent knows that Adam will find him out as a liar if go directly to him as he knew every beast by their characters hence he go for the woman.

Young observed that when the Bible says that Adam gave names to the animals it means far more than that he merely looked at animals and uttered some sound, possibly onomatopoeic in nature. In the Semitic languages to name something means to recognize and to mark out its essential nature and characteristic. When therefore Adam named that animal, he was classifying and categorizing inasmuch as he was created in the image of God and consequently possessed the faculty both of thought and speech he was able to name the animals. He knows what they exist for . . ." [6]

Since Adam and Eve chose to obey Satan (and disobeyed God) who come in the subtlety of the serpent and ate of the forbidden fruit thereby make God their Creator a liar, sin entered in to the word, for indeed their eyes were opened to know evil. Though they did not die a physical death, they died spiritually and the glory of God covering them was removed hence they discovered they were naked.

Dixon in his book observes that the tragic story of the disobedience of humans unfolds in disaster. The woman, who had been created from the man, and is of the man eats first of the forbidden fruit. At the time she eats, she has been clearly deceived. She truly thinks she is doing a wise thing. All the ingredients of things most appealing to humans are present. The fruit is good food, it is pleasant to the eye, and there is wisdom to be had. What's wrong with that? There is nothing wrong with it if those three things are the total equation. There is, however, an additional factor. God said ' . . . thou shall not eat of it . . .' (Genesis 2:17). God's Word always outweighs human reasoning. [7]

Despite man's disobedience to Gods commandment and in their sinful nature, and when they could not even take care of themselves, God as a loving Father clothed Adam and Eve in their state of nudity which brings the first hope and promise of salvation to mankind. Hamilton said in his book, Genesis 3:15 has traditionally been viewed by Christians as the first word of promise-in a prophetic sense-of deliverance from sin. The provision of a covering for Adam and Eve is immediate in an eschatological context. Its concern is the future, not the present.[8]

In essence, when God clothed Adam and Eve after their disobedient, He entered into a promise of Salvation and redemption for mankind and this He does by sending the last Adam, the Lord Jesus Christ to come and redeemed mankind and serve as a ransom for the penalty of the sin committed by Adam and Eve.

The man now asserts his authority over his wife by naming her Eve, Heb. Hawwah-mother of all who live, wrote Davidson. He went on to explain that the name Hawwah becomes a symbol of hope. Even the midst of the divinely inflicted penalty of death, there is continuing life: here is the mother of who live.[8]

DID GOD WITHDRAW HIS PROMISE TO MAN?

After man was beguiled by the devil and fell from the original purpose of God, the only thing God did was to withdraw His fellowship in the garden from man as he (man) was driven out of the garden by the angel with the sword of flaming fire. Genesis 3:23-24. What a disgrace!

Because man failed does not mean God will not actualised His original plan, for the bible says;

> **"God is not a man, that He should lie; neither the son of man, that he should repent: hath he said, and shall he not do it? Or hath he spoken, and shall he not make it good?". Numbers 23:19.**

One of the characteristics of God is the ability NEVER to fail. God is a man of His word. Remember, after God finished His work of creation, He made a statement of been fulfilled, a statement of successful man who was looking forward for the "fruits" of His labour, therefore He could not afford to fail.

The devil who is the arch-enemy of man since his rebellion against God has been attacking the work of God; especially man. The devil is still out there looking for families to destroy and brings down the same way he tricked and beguiled Eve and brought chaos into her home. Do not give room to satanic temptations, husband and wife must avoid eating of any 'forbidden fruits' that can bring dire consequences. "Let marriage be held in honour among all, and let the bed be undefiled: but God will judge the sexually immoral and adulterers."(Hebrews 13:4).

Looking critically at the creation of man from the beginning and the commandment that God gave him to be fruitful and multiply, despite the sinful nature of man that led to his fall, God is still interested in the salvation of his children. It will be then be absurd to think the same God will allow any of His children to be barren.

Chapter Four

God Changed His Strategies

"God, wishing His elect to realize their own misery, often temporarily withdraws His favours: no more is needed to prove to us in a very short time what we really are." TERESA OF AVILA.

Every earthly father will always want the best for their children, even unto adulthood; assist them in every way possible, so is God our heavenly father. (Luke 11:10-13). God original plan for man and woman was to have everything with ease including the process of conception. Before the fall of man, God's commandment to man was to reproduce his kind, the method or way through which man and woman to fulfil this was not stated in the bible, thereby any assumption will just be fallacy and hypothesis. After man fell and was disgracefully sent out of the Garden of Eden, God placed a curse on the woman, who is going to be the 'channel' of these child bearing.

> **"Unto the woman he (God) said, I will greatly multiply thy sorrow and thy CONCEPTION; in sorrow thou shall bring forth children . . . " Genesis 3:16**

The word conception connotes pregnancy, which is to carry a baby in the uterus or the womb. God NEVER said to the woman that she will not conceive or simply put, be pregnant. He only said " . . . I will greatly multiply thy sorrow and thy CONCEPTION (pregnancy) . . ."

This implies that God—despite the sinful nature of man is still interested in man been "fruitful, multiplying and replenish the land" as originally scheduled though man had gone into apostasy. The only penalty was that man and his wife must need to be corrected and disciplined (not necessarily punished) for been disobedience and their act of treachery to prevent further re occurrence. But definitely not by become barren.

Chapter Five

Man As A Spirit Being

"We live at the threshold of a universal recognition that the human being is not mere matter, but a potent, energetic field of consciousness. Modalities of the past millennium are quickly giving way to breakthrough technologies wherein we heal ourselves at the level of all true healing, which is spirit."
Michael Beckwith

The first man, Adam was first formed as a spirit being. We should understand that when we say that God created man in His own image, we are not talking about the physical body or flesh that man has. God is a Spirit being.

John 4:24

> **24. God is a Spirit; and they that worship him must worship him in Spirit and in truth.**

Nobody has ever seen God in His full glory (not even Moses) because He is a Spirit Being and that is why Jesus said:

5. . . . verily, verily I say unto thee, Except a man be born of water and of the SPIRIT, he cannot enter into the kingdom of God.

6. That which is born of the flesh is flesh; and that which is born of SPIRIT is SPIRIT. John 3:5, 6.

These words of Jesus emphatically stated that before man will go back to God or have communication with Him, man must be in the Spirit. Why? Man is a Spirit being too, created in the image of God.

Rick Warren wrote in his book, the purpose driven life: "in all creation, only human beings are made "in God's image." This is a great privilege and gives us dignity. We don't know all this phrase covers, but we do know some of the aspects it includes: Like God, we are SPIRITUAL BEINGS-our spirits are immortal and will outlast our earthly bodies; we are intellectual-we can think, reason, and solve problems; like God, we are relational-we can give and receive real love; and we have a moral consciousness-we can discern right from wrong, which makes us accountable to God."[9]

Someone might ask, what about my body? The simple illustration is this: the body or the flesh is the 'housing' to say, where man dwells as a spirit. God wanted someone to fellowship with, to have a physical contact with not just a spirit.

27. So God created man in His own IMAGE, in the IMAGE of God created he him . . . Genesis 1:27

After man was created in the image of God, the good question to ask is where was man? The answer of course, in the spiritual realm, not in the physical for he has no body or physical form yet, but God see him alone in the spirit and that was not what He (God) wanted. He want someone to till the garden, take care of everything He created (remember God created the garden with all the plants, herbs before man was formed. Genesis 1:11-12) but a Spirit cannot do this. Let us examine this verse from the bible:

> **5. And every plant of the field before it was in the earth, and every herb of the field before it grew: for the Lord God had not caused it to rain upon the earth, and there was not A MAN to till the ground. Genesis 2:5**

God wanted man to till the ground but this verse says; " . . . and there was not A MAN to till the ground." But Genesis 1:27 says: "so God CREATED man in his own image . . ." If man has been 'created' earlier, as this scripture implies, where was man when God was looking for a man in Gen. 2:5 to till the ground? The simple answer is that man still exists as a spirit being.

Let us now examine what God has to do next to bring man into the physical being to become useful.

Genesis 2:7

> **7. And the Lord God FORMED man of the DUST of the ground, and he breathed into his nostril, the breath of life; AND MAN BECAME A LIVING SOUL.**

Now let us consider few words here, in Gen. 1:27 " . . . God CREATED man in his own image . . ." While in Gen. 2:7, the bible says "And the Lord God FORMED man of the dust of the ground . . ." Amazing!

To create according to Oxford Advanced Learner dictionary means:

- To cause something to EXIST; to make something NEW or ORIGINAL. Thus we learnt here that man was created in Genesis 1:27 as an EXISTENCE of the ORIGINAL God who is a Spirit being without form.

To form by the same dictionary means:

- The EXTERNAL appearance of somebody or something;

- The SHAPE of somebody or something.

To form now as stated in Genesis 2:7 means that God wanted a SHAPE for man for the purpose of tilling and some other things (sexual intercourse?). So God in His infinite wisdom and craftsmanship now gathered the dust of the ground together, draw a picture of how he want the man to look in the physical, and breathe the SPIRIT inside the moulded image and called it man. That explains to us that the physical body is not really the man but EXTERNAL appearance of the real man inside. Myles Munroe writes: "to understand the purpose of the body, we must understand the purpose of man. When God created man, He created him a spirit being with physical house (body) . . . the human body was thus specifically designed to relate to and pick up the earth or physical realm."[10]

God as a master craftsman and in His infinite wisdom, knows that a spirit cannot give birth to children. He decided to form an external body for man in order to fulfil the promise of procreation. You are wonderfully and fearfully made by God. He took every care to form your organs and every bits of your body. Everything that God created is without blemish. You are created to have your own children.

Chapter Six

Purpose Of The External Body

"The body is your temple. Keep it pure and clean for the soul to reside in." Iyengar

> *"The body too has its rights; and it will have them: they cannot be trampled on without peril. The body ought to be the soul's best friend. Many good men however have neglected to make it such: so it has become a fiend and has plagued them." Augustus William Hare and Julius Charles Hare*

After a successful 'house' or an 'external' appearance had been given to man, he has a purpose to fulfil with this body. Remember I said earlier that before the fall of man, the Bible never says how God intended for man to "conceive, multiply, and reproduce after their own kind." But one thing that is certain is this; the reproductive organs that man has since God formed him with the dust of the ground before he was deceived by the devil and fall are the same reproductive organs he has after the fall. There is nowhere in the Bible that suggests God changed the physical appearance of both man and woman.

The organs and structures of the male reproductive system give men the ability to fertilize a woman's ovum (egg) to produce a baby.

Several different organs and structures make up the male reproductive system. These include the testes, where sperm is made, several ducts (tubes) where sperm is stored, and the penis. The penis has a single duct called the urethra; this releases both sperm and urine. Also included in the male reproductive system are the accessory sex glands, which include the prostate gland and seminal vesicles. These glands make special fluids, which are added to sperm as it travels through the ducts. Together the liquid is known as semen.

Hormones are also made by parts of a man's reproductive system.

The testes start developing inside the internal body cavity in a growing baby (fetus). About two months before a male baby is born the testes start to descend into the scrotal sacs. Because they are outside the main body cavity the testes are slightly cooler. This difference in temperature helps sperm production.

The penis contains the urethra, which passes both urine and semen. There are three main parts of the penis, the root, body and glans. The root is the part attached to the lower abdomen. The body of the penis is made up of a spongy type of tissue, which swells when blood enters during an erection. The glans penis is the slightly larger area towards the end of the penis and contains the opening of the urethra.

What does the male reproductive system do?

Its main function is to give men the ability to fertilize a woman's ovum by producing and delivering semen. The testes also make hormones which help men develop the characteristics associated with being male. This includes the distribution of pubic hair, enlargement of the penis and deepening of the voice.

How does the male reproductive system work?

During puberty, levels of certain hormones in the brain begin to increase. These changes cause an increase in the production and release of two hormones from the pituitary gland—luteinizing hormone (LH) and follicle-stimulating hormone (FSH). (The pituitary gland is a small gland at the base of the brain. It makes various hormones which are released into the bloodstream including LH and FSH.) LH in the bloodstream causes cells in the testes to make and release testosterone, another hormone. Some of this testosterone gets converted into another form. Together, the two forms of testosterone help to develop and enlarge the penis and other male sex organs. Testosterone also helps to encourage muscle and skeletal growth and deepen the male voice.

FSH and testosterone work together to stimulate the testes to produce sperm. Each sperm cell takes between 65-75 days to form, and around 300 million are produced every day. Inside the testes sperm is made in structures called the seminiferous tubules. At the top and to the back of each testis is the epididymis, which stores sperm.

Leading from the epididymis is the vas deferens. The vas deferens carries sperm to the penis. To do this the vas deferens passes into the internal cavity of the body. Passing close to the bladder the vas deferens eventually enters the prostate gland where the tube becomes the urethra.

The prostate gland lies just beneath the bladder. It is normally about the size of a chestnut. The prostate gland makes a specialized fluid which is added to sperm during ejaculation. The seminal vesicles also add fluid to the sperm during ejaculation.

The mixture of sperm, fluid from the prostate and fluid from the seminal vesicles is called semen. About 60-70% of the volume of semen comes from the seminal vesicles. The urethra (the tube which transports urine and semen) runs through the middle of the prostate.

When sexually aroused a number of changes occur inside the penis. The arteries supplying the penis expand allowing more blood to enter its tissues. The increase in blood flow causes the penis to enlarge. The extra blood flow plus signals from the nervous system and chemical changes cause an erection. Ejaculation (the contractions that release semen) is a reflex action, which means it is not consciously controlled. As part of the reflex action, the opening that drains the bladder is closed. This means that urine is not released at the same time as semen. The volume of semen in a typical ejaculation is between 2.5-5 milliliters (mL) with more than 20 million sperm per ML.[11]

The female reproductive anatomy includes internal and EXTRNAL structures. The function of the external female reproductive structures (the genitalia) is to enable sperm to enter the body. The main external structures of the female reproductive system include:

* **Labia majora:** The labia majora enclose and protect the other external reproductive organs. Literally translated as "large lips," the labia majora are relatively large and fleshy, and are comparable to the scrotum in males. The labia majora contain sweat and oil-secreting glands. After puberty, the labia majora are covered with hair.

* **Labia minora:** Literally translated as "small lips," the labia minora can be very small or up to 2 inches wide. They lie just inside the labia majora, and surround the openings to the vagina (the canal that joins the lower part of the uterus to the outside of the body) and urethra (the tube that carries urine from the bladder to the outside of the body).

* **Bartholin's glands:** These glands are located next to the vaginal opening and produce a fluid (mucus) secretion.

* **Clitoris:** The two labia minora meet at the clitoris, a small, sensitive protrusion that is comparable to the penis in males. The clitoris is covered by a fold of skin, called the prepuce, which is similar to the foreskin at the end of the penis. Like the penis, the clitoris is very sensitive to stimulation and can become erect.

The internal reproductive organs include:

* **Vagina:** The vagina is a canal that joins the cervix (the lower part of uterus) to the outside of the body. It also is known as the birth canal.

* **Uterus (womb):** The uterus is a hollow, pear-shaped organ that is the home to a developing fetus. The uterus is divided into two parts: the cervix, which is the lower part that opens into the vagina, and the main body of the uterus, called the corpus. The corpus can easily expand to hold a developing baby. A channel through the cervix allows sperm to enter and menstrual blood to exit.

* **Ovaries:** The ovaries are small, oval-shaped glands that are located on either side of the uterus. The ovaries produce eggs and hormones.

*   **Fallopian tubes:** These are narrow tubes that are attached to the upper part of the uterus and serve as tunnels for the ova (egg cells) to travel from the ovaries to the uterus. Conception, the fertilization of an egg by a sperm, normally occurs in the fallopian tubes. The fertilized egg then moves to the uterus, where it implants to the uterine wall.[12]

How inconclusive and incorrect will it be to imagine that after God have taken time to put all these delicate organs and system in place in your body for the sole purpose of reproduction and for Him now to withhold them from functioning? This is the gimmick and deception of the devil to lure you away from the promise and covenant of God. Hold on unto His Words of promise and you will never be put to shame.

Chapter Seven

The Act Of Connubial

"Do not refuse and deprive and defraud each other [of your marital rights], except perhaps by mutual consent for a time, so that you may devote yourselves unhindered to prayer. But afterwards resume marital relations, lest Satan tempt you [to sin] through lack of restraint of sexual desire." 1 Corinthians 7: 5 {AMP}

Immediately after man disobeyed God, ate of the forbidden fruit commanded against eating, the Bible says:

"And the eyes of them both were opened, and they knew that they were NAKED . . ." Genesis 3:7

Somebody might be asking, 'was Adam and Eve blind before they ate the fruit?' No, not physically anyway. This means the man and the woman became conscious of their bodies, the duo now realised that some of their body parts differs from each other. Simply put, the man and the woman became aware of their sexes and become sexually attractive to each other. Gen. 3:7-8

I strongly believe that one of the reasons why man and his mate was hurriedly chase out of the Garden of Eden was because they have become wise and were aware of their sexes.

"And the Lord God said, Behold the man is become as one of us, to know the GOOD and EVIL . . . " Genesis 3:22

They now understand the functions of their body parts (especially the genitals) and before they could defile the Garden (though we never know how God intended for man to reproduce after his kind with his wife. We cannot know everything, God alone is omniscience.) He sent them out. Gen. 3:23, 24.

The man and woman after been driven out of the Garden of Eden, starts coexisting together, this starts the beginning of the fulfilment of the original plan and commandment of God to " . . . Be fruitful, and multiply, and replenish the earth . . . " Gen. 1:28

How Does Conception Takes Place?

The process of conception and pregnancy are complex – starting from the fertilization of the egg by a single spermatozoon which is a mature male germ cell to the fertilization of the ova in the uterine wall. A single spermatozoon is microscopic in size and has a flat elliptical head containing a spherical centre section, and a long tail by which it swims.

Spermatozoa (plural) are produced in the somniferous tubules of the testes. When matured, usually when a man is between the ages of nine and fourteen the spermatozoa are carried in the semen. At the peak of sexual intercourse, the semen is discharged or released into the vagina of the female. A single discharge which is about teaspoonful of semen may contain over 250 million spermatozoa of which only a few of these will make it to the fallopian tubes and just one will fertilize an ovum, if present.

The ovum is the female reproductive or germ cell which after fertilization is capable of developing into a new member of the same species scientifically known as mitosis.

Following ejaculation, the sperm must transport themselves through the cervix and into the fallopian tube where fertilization will take place and back into the womb or uterus where the baby is nurtured and nursed between the periods of 38 to 42 weeks.

God Fulfilled His Promise

> **"And Adam KNEW his wife; and she conceived, and bare Cain and said, I have gotten a man from the Lord."**
> **Genesis 4:1 (KJV)**

The word 'KNEW' in the above scripture is synonymous to 'have sexual relationship', thus the passage could read "And Adam have sexual relationship with his wife."

The New American Standard put it this way: **"Now the man had RELATIONS with his wife Eve, and she conceived . . . "**
Gen. 4:1(NASB)

The New International put it this way: **"ADAM LAY with his wife Eve, and she became pregnant and gave birth to Cain . . . "**
Gen 4:1 (NIV)

All the above scripture extracts, 'knew', 'had relationship', 'lay' expressed the same thing which is to have sexual intercourse. In fact The New Living Translation confirms this: **"Now Adam had sexual relation with his wife, Eve, and she became pregnant." Gen. 4:1 (NLT)**

This process of producing after 'his kind' by the man and the woman is known scientifically as sexual reproduction.

Chapter Eight

Sexual Reproduction And Birth

You are all beautiful, my love.
There is no spot in you.
Come with me from Lebanon, my bride,
With me from Lebanon.
Look from the top of Amana,
From the top of Senir and Hermon,
From the lions' dens,
From the mountains of the leopards.
You have ravished my heart, my sister, my bride.
You have ravished my heart with one of your eyes,
With one chain of your neck.
How beautiful is your love, my sister, my bride!
How much better is your love than wine!
The fragrance of your perfumes than all manner of spices!
Your lips, my bride, drip like the honeycomb.
Honey and milk are under your tongue.
The smell of your garments is like the smell of Lebanon.
A locked up garden is my sister, my bride;
A locked up spring,
A sealed fountain.
Your shoots are an orchard of pomegranates, with precious fruits:

Henna with spikenard plants,
Spikenard and saffron,
Calamus and cinnamon, with every kind of incense tree;
Myrrh and aloes, with all the best spices,
A fountain of gardens,
A well of living waters,
Flowing streams from Lebanon." Song Of Solomon 3:7-15. [WEB)

Some mammals (mammals are any class of animals that give birth to live babies and feed their young on milk from the breast. e.g. Man) produce their own kinds by sexual reproduction. According to Rao and Kaur "sexual reproduction is a type of reproduction in which both sexes, the male and the female, are involved. Most animals and higher plants multiply by sexual reproduction. It is the production of offspring by the fusion of genetic material contained in the sex cells or gamete."[13]

The man and the woman are equipped with sexual reproductive organs to produce their own kinds. We can hereby define sexual reproduction as the ability of a woman to become pregnant with a baby after having sexual relations for the purpose of giving birth (bring forth) to a child.

These also imply that God wants every man and woman to have their children and not necessarily to adopt one. The idea of gay and lesbian couples was never part of God's plan for His children hence He created us male and female.

The man and the woman has to become mature enough before they can mutually consent together to become husband and wife for this great task. God does not allow and is still frowning against premarital sex and sex among young teens.

"Flee sexual immorality!" Every sin that a man does is outside the body, "but he who commits sexual immorality sins against his own body. Or don't you know that your body is a temple of the Holy Spirit which is in you, which you have from God? You are not your own, for you were bought with a price. Therefore glorify God in your body and in your spirit, which are God's." 1Corinthians 6:18-20 {WEB}

The same God who created the reproductive organs in both the male and the females and commanded man to be fruitful has the ability to see to the conception of healthy and godly children. Sexual intercourse is solely designed for married couples and not between teenagers and young adults who are not married. Sex must not be used as a weapon of oppression or be abused. We should not yield our body to sinful lust and be faithful that He will bring His Word to pass in your lives. Amen.

"Let marriage be held in honour among all, and let the marriage bed be unpolluted; for fornicators and adulterers God will judge." Hebrews 13:4 {WEYMOUTH}

Chapter Nine

The Will Of God In Christian Marriage

"By our Heavenly Father and only because of God, only because of God. We're like other couples. We do not get along perfectly; we do not go without arguments and, as I call them, fights, and heartache and pain and hurting each other. But a marriage is three of us."
Barbara Mandrel

I cannot but express how significantly important it is to mention here what the wills of God are in a godly and Christian's marriage. If and when these wills are fulfilled by the couple, they can be rest assured that God Himself will arise to destroy every yoke of barrenness in their home.

God commanded that only people that are joined together as husband and wife have the legal right to have sexual relationship. Gen.2:23-25. Any violators of this commandment will be strictly punished as necessary.

Do not take for granted the fact that it is God's wish and commandment that man " . . . be fruitful, multiply and replenish the earth . . . " to start yielding your members for immoral and uncontrolled sexual lust. Roman 6:13-19.

"And the Lord God said, it is not good that the man should be alone; I will make a help meet for him." Genesis 2:18

The above scripture clearly define the motive for which God institute marriage. The institution of the family and marriage is the oldest human institution. Most people of the world who belong to the monotheist religion, that is those who believe in the existence of one Supreme, Omnipotent intelligent God, believe that the family/ marriage is as old as Adam and Eve. Consistent with this faith, the first recorded married couple in history are Adam and Eve.

Adam was very delighted to have Eve as a life partner. Upon seen Eve, he exclaimed in awe admiration **" . . . this is now the bone of my bones and flesh of my flesh . . . " Genesis 2:23a.**

Marriage can hereby be define as a bond between a man and a woman, entered into willingly, usually by mutual consent, a commitment of self, the giving voluntary of oneself to a partner of the opposite sex for life. Genesis 24:56-58.

Marriage is an institution, and like every institutions marriage has its special characteristics and its governing rules.

Consent: Mutual consent is one of the basic elements of a happy marriage. It involves the voluntary and mutual exchange of rights and obligation within marriage. As a rule, marriage should not be forced on any party. Both parties (including parents) must consent to the marriage or there would be resentments, bitterness, a lot of stress and unhappiness.

UNITY: Marriage is a union between a man and a woman and there must be an unbreakable bond between the husband and wife. Gen.

2:22—324. There must be no room for a third party and absolute fidelity is demanded. Married couples need to act with oneness of heart and mind and to be faithful to each other. Sebastian in the book 'ministers and ministries in the local church:' stated that "unity signifies an exclusive conjugal relationship between one man and one woman (Mk 10:6-8). In marriage a man and a woman mutually give and accept each other. To include anyone else within this privilege sphere of marital intimacy violates the unity proper to marriage. Without unity the total self-giving essential to marriage is impossible. It, therefore, excludes all forms of polygamy, where one woman has several husbands."[14]

Another reason God want man to get married is for the purpose of holiness. Rev. Arriola observes that "Matrimony is a sacrament that celebrates the union between a man and a woman bound by Christ and His church to a union that is to last until death. It is a call to two baptized people to serve as a light to one another in order to achieve the perfection of holiness."[15] God is holy and wants man to be holy too hence He is frowned at any form of sexual indiscipline.

God has never been, and will never be the author of gay marriages. A godly marriage existed and is consummated between two people of the opposite sex and not between people of the same sex. Homosexuality and gay marriage does not starts in our modern day, it was a common practice by the people of Sodom and Gomorrah and that is why no record of that country is anywhere to be find today as God destroyed them for this single act of homosexuality. James Brundage writes: "two passages in Leviticus prohibit sexual relationships between men, and one of them prescribed the death penalty for same-sex intercourse . . .

the rabbinical commentators certainly considered homosexuality activity a serious crime that merited death by stoning . . . "[16]

Procreation which is the basis for this book is another reasons God want man and woman to be joined together as husband and wife. Donald Asci in his book 'The conjugal act as personal act' writes "procreation is the primary purpose of the sexual faculty and the primary end of the conjugal act, but what is procreation according to Pius XII? In the teachings of Pius XII procreation and biological reproduction differ greatly, principally because of the personal nature of procreation. Procreation involves more than the physical elements entailed in the transmission of life because it results from a specific free choice of a man and a woman. In procreating man and woman choose to cooperate with God and nature precisely as persons . . . in releasing the force of life."[17]

Whether as a newly married couple or an old one, the way to live a fulfilled and victorious marital life and enjoys the will of God in marriage is by been adherent and addictive to the Words of God. The Bible is the only manual guidance to a successful conjugal bliss. James 1:21-22.

Below are some 'forces' that must be put in place to have a fulfilled marital life.

THE FORCE OF FORGIVENESS: Husband and wife are like the proverbial 'tongue and teeth' that must learn to live together peacefully. While the 'teeth' is chewing and the 'tongue' is helping to 'lubricate' what is been chewed, most often the 'teeth' will mistakenly bite the 'tongue', but strangely the 'tongue' has never leave the mouth or stop assisting the 'teeth'. Matt. 6:14-15. The couple must learn to forgive one another when conflicts arise.

THE FORCE OF MUTUAL RELATIONSHIP: The wife must learn to be submissive to the husband and the husband on the other hand must love his wife. Do everything together in harmony, trust and in love.

> "Two are better than one, because they have a good reward for their labour. [10]For if they fall, the one will lift up his fellow; but woe to him who is alone when he falls, and doesn't have another to lift him up. [11]Again, if two lie together, then they have warmth; but how can one keep warm alone? [12]If a man prevails against one who is alone, two shall withstand him; and a threefold cord is not quickly broken." Eccl. 4:9-12.

THE FORCE OF OPEN GOVERMENT: The government at home (like every institution) must never be that of oligarchy. This is a government run by father with children with exclusive of the mother or vice versa.

Anarchy must not be practiced in a marriage, this is whereby only the man or the woman take sole actions, execute decisions and judgement without consulting with the partner. (Do as I say!)

THE FORCE OF FAITH: Hebrews 11:6 says "for without faith it is impossible to please Him (God) . . ." The same way it is going to be difficult for a couple that does not have faith in God and in one another to live pleasant and fruitful lives. Have faith in God that as He has brought you together as a couple, He can as well make it possible for you to have your children.

THE FORCE OF ENDURANCE: Heb. 6:13-15. The endurance I am talking about here must not be mistaken for suffering, hardship or when there is case of abuse. God does not intend marriage to be 'endure' but to be enjoyed. Reading Heb. 6:13-15 closely,

"For when God made promise to Abraham, because he could swear by no greater, he sware by himself, Saying, Surely blessing I will bless thee, and multiplying I will multiply thee. And so, after he had patiently endured, he obtained the promise. For men verily swear by the greater: and an oath for confirmation *is* to them an end of all strife."

God made a promise to Abraham the he will be blessed. The Bible now says " . . . after he had patiently endured, he obtained the promise." To endure in marriage simply means to:

- Wait patiently on one another and God.

- To be tolerant of each other's behaviours and shortcoming.

- To continue to live together happily even in the face of challenges of life. The mere fact that God want couple to have a happy marital life does not rule out occasional challenges. E.g. Delayed conception.

THE FORCES OF PRAYER AND FASTING: One of the weapons God has given unto the couples to deal with forces of darkness is prayer and when combined with fasting is a missile that left the forces of darkness shattered. When husband and wife learn to combine prayer and fasting together, They will lead a perfect marital life. (Mark 9:25-29).

God, through Apostle Paul admonish the couple not to use all their time eating and enjoying 'honeymoon' but should abstained from one another for a season to give themselves to prayer and fasting especially when face with the challenge of delayed conception. (1Cor. 7:5). Learn to pray together and trust absolutely in God.

THE FORCE OF THE WORD: the foundation of your marriage must be Biblical based. (Psalm 119:105,130). All decision making, actions to be taken, business proposition, choice of carrier and how to have sexual relationship must be Word based. This is when you can have good successful marriage. Search daily and read Words of God as written in the Bible that promised us of been fruitful in child-bearing and meditate on them.

THE FORCE OF LOVE: Love is the foundation of this world, and its existence is primarily because of love. (John 3:16). Couples must therefore learn to establish their home on love. Looking at the book of (1Corinthians 13:1-8), the word translated 'charity' (KJV) in the original Greek letter is 'agape' meaning Love i.e. affection or benevolence.

Love can thereby be explained as:

* Love is patient and kind.

* Love is not jealous or boastful or proud or rude.

* Love is not a *dictator.*

* Love is not irritable.

* Love *forgives* and forgets, does not keep record of wrong doing.

* Love never gives up, never loses *faith.*

* Love is always hopeful, and endures through every circumstance.

Note that all the forces we have treated earlier, all revolves around love. Let the love of God guide you through the time you are expecting the fruits of the womb. The husband should not be nagging and unaffectionate towards his wife. The wife on the other hand should not be unnecessarily suspicious of the husband when seeing with other women.

THE FORCES OF DELIGIENCE/OR HARDWORKING

"But if any man provide not for his own house, he hath denied the faith, and is WORSE than an infidel." 1Timothy 5:8.

Apostle Paul was not referring to man alone in this scripture, he was addressing both husband and wife. How do I mean? Proverbs 31:10-27 talks about the duty and responsibilities of the wife in taking care and providing basic necessity for her home. Man as the head of the family must endeavour to work very hard, (not been lazy or idle) to take care of his family. (Proverbs 22:29).

The wife on the other hand, must not company with 'full housewives', who do nothing and put all the family responsibilities solely on their husbands. She must be doing something to assist and encourage the husband, after all for this purpose (to be a help mate) God originally created her. (Genesis 2:18).

Couples (not husband alone) who could not take care of their 'own' (children, relatives, church of God, etc.) " . . . hath denied the faith and are worse than infidel". Imagine a scenario where the woman is a House-wife, and the husband is a House-man, the family will definitely eat House-flies!

THE FORCE OF UNDERSTANDING: To understand simply means to know the meaning of WORDS, A LANGUAGE, and A PERSON'S CHARACTER.

* WORDS: Husband and wife must understand, knows the meaning of each other spoken words. Every words must

be carefully weighed before spoken, and must be for the edification of their home. Idle talks, gossiping, profanity must be avoided. Ephesians 4:29.

* LANGUAGE: This includes facial expression, body expression, making of sound (grunt, hissed, sighing, murmuring, etc.). All these must be noted understood and necessary actions taken when manifested. For example, a husband that comes back home from work and continue to sigh repeatedly with a sad and confused countenance must be an immediate concern of the wife. She should know instinctively that something is amiss without been told.

* PERSONS'S CHARACTER: The fact that husband and wife comes from different (in most cases) ethnic, cultural and family background, are enough reasons to be tolerance of one and other and correct in love some characters that each might find offensive. Couples must take time to learn, adjust and adapt to each other characters. Do not attempt to impose behaviour on your spouse because your friends' wife or husband has that trait, instead learn to appreciate your spouse and in love go together to the school of 'self-discovery'.

Chapter Ten

Adam And Eve Fulfilled The Promise

"You shall be blessed above all peoples; there shall not be male or female barren among you, or among your cattle."
Deuteronomy 7:14 {AMP}

"Everyone admits that the male is the primary efficient cause in generation, as being that in whom the species or form resides, and they further assert that his genitures emitted in coitus causes the egg both to exist and to be fertile. But how the semen of the cock produces the chick from the egg, neither the philosophers nor the physicians of yesterday or today have satisfactorily explained, or solved the problem formulated by Aristotle." William Harvey.

After Adam and Eve were chased out of Eden, they begins to fulfil the commandment of God, they begin to reproduce their own kinds.

Genesis 4:1

And Adam knew Eve his wife; and she conceived, and bare CAIN, and said I have gotten a man from the Lord.

This was a statement of fact from Eve after giving birth to her *first male* child, (not first born child). She looked at the feature of the baby and discovered it was like that of her husband, Adam.

I said *first male* child, because she must have been given birth to girls before, (who has the same feature as her) hence her remark " . . . I have gotten a MAN from the Lord . . ."

The Amplified bible renders it this way:

> **AND ADAM knew Eve his wife, and she became pregnant and bore Cain; and she said, I have gotten *and* gained a man with the help of Lord. Genesis 4:1 (AMP)**

The word 'and' that was written in italic means an addition to something that has been happening or happened before. Eve had been having female children before. She knew they were girls because they have same features as hers, but immediately she got Cain she can't just but exclaimed . . . "I have gotten *and* gained man (i.e. this time around it is a man) with the help of the Lord" Gen.4:1.

How do I know this? It is in the custom of the ancient Jews/ Israelites not to record the birth of a female child. Let us examine some scriptures to base my argument.

Exodus 2:1-4

1. **And there went a man of the house of Levi, and took to wife a daughter of Levi.**

2. **And the woman conceived, and bares a son: and when she saw him that he was a goodly child, she hid him three months.**

3. **And when she could no longer hide him, she took for him an ark of bulrushes, and daubed it with slime and pitch and the child therein; and she laid it in the flags by the river's bank.**

4. **And his *SISTER* stood afar off, to wit what would be done to him.**

The above scripture starts in verse one with a man and a woman from the tribe of Levi who were married to each other. Verse two started with the birth of a MALE child (Moses), who was born to the family. As a matter of fact, verse two made it look as if this MALE child was their first child; but when you read verse four, it says "And his *SISTER* stood afar off . . ." We should know of course that this sister could not have been his younger sister as " . . . she stood afar off . . ." This can only describe a grown up sister.

Now the point is this, if not that the MALE child's sister (later known as Mariam) has a significant role to play in this story, we might not have known for sure that Moses had a sister for the story of this family starts with the birth of Moses and not of the sister.

Secondly, the patriarch Jacob gave birth to thirteen children, but in the history of Jews, we only read and hear of twelve patriarchs who represent the twelve tribes of Israel. What happened to the thirteenth child? She was a woman. She cannot become a leader of a tribe.

To substantiate my argument further, when you read through the book of Genesis chapter one to chapter four, the first place a woman was noticed and made reference to beside Eve was in Genesis chapter 4 verses 17.

Genesis 4:17

> And Cain knew his WIFE; and she conceived, and bare
> Enoch . . . . "

The good question we need to ask is where does the WIFE of Cain come from? The bible or the writer of this story never stated that God created another being or woman beside Adam and Eve. The answer is this: the wives referred to both in verse 17 for Cain and others in verse 18, and 19 respectively could only have been the first set of *girls* that Eve gave birth to before Cain! God allowed the family to marry one another to fulfil his commandment before the new Law of opposing marriage from the same family was later given to Moses.

Throughout the Old Testament and The New Testament of the Bible, since man starts to reproduce his own kind, nobody was recorded barren for ever (those that was mentioned were for a short period as we shall learn later). As a matter of fact, as men begins to increase and filled the face of the earth (even after the demise of Adam, the first man that God gave the commandment to) God continue to reassure His people about His desire for them to be fruitful, multiply, and replenish the earth. Deuteronomy 28:8-13.

The few women that were recorded barren were for a few years which were permitted by God for one reasons or the other. Well! He is a sovereign God! All these women were later reported to conceived and bare children because God can never go back on His Word.

Deuteronomy 7:14

> **Thou shall be blessed above all people: there shall not be male
> or female BARREN among you, or among your cattle.**

If God never wants our cattle to be barren, how could he have break His own words concerning His children.

Chapter Eleven

The Commandment Becomes A Covenant

"Marriage has a unique place because it speaks of an absolute faithfulness, a covenant between radically different persons, male and female; and so it echoes the absolute covenant of God with his chosen, a covenant between radically different partners."
Rowan D. Williams

Man has indeed begins to fill the faces of the earth. Many had been born and gone back to be with the Lord, but one fact still remains—God commandment to mankind to be fruitful, to multiply, replenish the earth and produce their kind never ceased as this commandment was for the first man Adam and all his offspring.

After the demise of Adam, God in a way of reassuring man established the same commandment of *fruitfulness* now in a form of **covenant** with somebody else.

Genesis 17:1-6

1. And when Abram was ninety years old and nine, the Lord appeared to Abram, and said unto him, I am the Almighty God; walk before me, and be thou perfect.

2. And I will make *my covenant* between me and thee, and I will *multiply* thee exceedingly.

3. And Abram fell on his face: and God talked with him saying,

4. As for me, behold, my covenant is with thee, *and thou shalt be a father of many nations.*

5. Neither shall thy name any more be called Abram, but thy name shall be Abraham; for a father of many nations have I made thee.

6. *And I will make thee exceeding fruitful*, and I will make nations of thee, and kings shall come out of thee, *and KINGS* shall come out of thee.

The new man that found favour with God to renew His commandment with but now based on covenant was Abram (whose name was later changed to Abraham).

Covenant is a Hebrew term *berit,* which is commonly associated with *beritu,* a noun from Akkadian which simply means 'bond' or 'fetter. The word covenant was mentioned some 285 times in the Old Testament alone which actually suggests that it express the idea of deeply serious commitments between God and Man.[18]

There are altogether about seven covenants that are most significant in the Bible and as agreed by some renowned scholars; The Adamic covenant, The Noahic covenant, The Abrahamic covenant, The Priestly covenant, The Mosaic covenant, The Davidic covenant as well as the New covenant. All these covenants are interwoven, for one came after the other might have failed and failure to study them together might not give us a better understanding of these covenants, but for the purpose of this book I will be talking about the Abrahamic covenant.

The Abrahamic covenant is a covenant of faith and of promise between God and Abraham by which God is unconditionally bound to make Abraham and his descendants a great nation, to be a blessing to all the families of the earth and by which the Lord Jesus Christ will emerge. Adam dies with his covenant; the Abrahamic covenant I believe is an expansion and continuation of Adamic covenant. God gave this covenant to fulfil his intention of restoring humanity back unto him. Genesis 12:2-3. Circumcision which is the cutting away of the flesh of the foreskin serves as a token of reminder of this covenant and involves shedding of blood. Circumcision represented the cutting away of the flesh, of the old, in order to embrace the new.[19] Abraham was chosen to be the father of all that believe according to Roman 4:16. And the scripture, foreseeing that God would justify the earth through faith, (in the only begotten Son of God)

The covenant between Abraham and God was not in any way different from His original commandment given to the first man-Adam-to be fruitful (vs6), to multiply (vs2), and to replenish the earth (vs4, 5) father of many nations. Elizabeth Mark believes that the divine promise of fruitfulness had been one of the premises and signs of the covenant that had set Abraham and Sarah on from the land of their ancestors toward and unknown destiny.[20]

Another spectacular promise that God added to Abraham was that not only will he be exceedingly fruitful and multiply, Kings will come out of his great grandchildren. What a promise! If God was and is (for the promise is eternal) interested in making Kings out of man, how wrong will it be to insinuate that this same God will shut the womb of any woman (forever) through which these promised kings will come. God never contradict Himself.

Chapter Twelve

Who Is Michal?

We begin to read the story of Michal from the book of 1 Samuel chapter 18. By now, as at the time this event took place, One of these promised Kings was a man called Saul; as a matter of fact he was the first King of Israel, (1Kings 9:1-27) and one of his daughters was this Michal we are talking about.

It got to a certain time that King Saul who was appointed by God Himself stop walking in obedience with God. That is not our story anyway, but again, in the armies of King Saul there was a young soldier called David who single handed wrought deliverance for Israel from the hand of Philistines. This single act of bravery and patriotism endear the young man David to the King who had earlier promised to give her daughter Merab (not Michal) out in marriage to David. 1Sam. 18:17

Although this was a secret plot by King Saul to kill David when he realised that the people loved David more than himself-the King. 1 Sam. 18:16. Another reason King Saul wanted David dead at all cost was the fact known to him later that God had chosen the young man (David) to be King is his stead. (1 Sam. 16:1-14).

The first plot to kill David failed, and instead for King Saul to give his daughter-Merab as wife unto David as earlier promised, she was given to another man called Adriel, a man from Meholathite. 1 Sam. 18:19 (they are inhabitant of Abel-meholah, meaning meadow of dancing. It was located in the Jordan valley, about 10 miles South of Beth-shean. Judges 7:22. 1Kings 4:12. It was the home of Elisa the prophet. 1Kings 19:16)

It was this Michal, another daughter to King Saul (probably a younger sister to Merab) that first loved David, I believe unknown to him. (1 Sam.18:20) When Michal love for David was rehearsed before King Saul-her father, he saw another way of using Michal his daughter as a trap to ensnare David. How? He thought by marrying Michal to David, he will get help from her to assassinate David. (1 Sam.18:20-21).

The plot to kill David failed after he had eventually married Michal, for Michal loved David so much that she refused to betray him to her father when he sent his assassin to kill David. (1 Sam. 19:11-17).

We should take cognizance of the fact that David and Michal was barely married when this incident happened and David later becomes a fugitive. From chapter 20 of the book of 1 Samuel, we discovered that David became a political fugitive wandering from one place to another for his dear life. So we can conclude that Michal was not with David all this time and there was no chance of her been impregnated by David.

I wish to state here that the husband and wife should always find time for each other. Do not allow your job, meetings even church activities to deny you the presence of one another. Couples must get to know more of one another and get to know their differences better as they spend quality times together. Ask and answer all questions with honesty. Do not allow members of either family to take much of your time, and as you stay together waiting patiently on God be rest assured that He will visit you as He visited Hannah.

Chapter Thirteen

Michal-Had No Child But Not Barren

"Never, surely, were man and wife more unequally yoked together than was David, the man after God's own heart, with Michal, Saul's daughter. What was David's meat was Michal's poison. What was sweeter than honey to David was gall and wormwood to Michal. The things that had become dearer and dearer to David's heart every day, those were the very things that drove Michal absolutely mad; furiously and ungovernably mad that day on which the ark of God was brought up to the city of David." David and Tamara

After so many battles between David and King Saul, (2Sam.3:1-2) several attempts were made to slay David but God gave him victory over King Saul who later died on the same day alongside his son Jonathan a very good friend of David. (1 Sam. 31:1-6).

With the death of King Saul and the throne empty, David returned back from his self-exile and because he was loved by the people for his good military record, he was unanimously made the next King. (2 Sam. 5:1-4). Expectedly, with all the victory that God give to David with his elevation to the throne as a King, and having regained the lost ark of covenant of God. One can imagine how elated and excited he will be. David was over joyous and danced before the Lord God in a way nobody else has done before especially someone in his position as a King. (2 Sam. 6:15).

Before we go further with that, we should note that immediately David came back from exile, he requested for his wife Michal to be restored back to him.

2Samuel 3:13

> And he said, Well; I will make a league with thee: but one thing I require of thee, that is, Thou shalt not see my face, except thou first bring Michal Saul's daughter, when thou comest to see my face.

This was David's response to Abner, the chief captain to late King Saul who now sent a truce message to King David desiring peace. Why did King David say " . . . except thou first bring Michal Saul's daughter . . ." and not " . . . except thou first bring Michal my wife . . ."? The answer is that all the years that David was in exile; his wife was given to another man in marriage!

2Samuel 3:14-16

> 14. And David sent messengers to Ishbosheth Saul's son, saying, Deliver me my wife Michal, which I espoused to me for an hundred foreskins of the Philistines.
>
> 15. And Ishbosheth sent, and took her from her HUSBAND, even from Phaltiel the son of Laish.
>
> 16. And her husband went with her along weeping behind her to Bahurim. Then said Abner unto him, Go, return. And he returned.

Now, we understand that Michal was re-united with David her first husband. One thing I got to notice though is that Michal did not re-unite with David of her own free will, though it was Michal that first expressed her love towards David and loved him so much she would not betrayed him.Michal who first expressed her love towards David and loved him so much she would not betrayed him.

Michal sudden aversion for David could be that she thought she was abandoned for so many years by David while he was in exile. In their book, David and Tamara explained that the last scene in Michal figures (2 Sam. 6:16-23) presents a contrast to the time as a result of love for David, flung aside conventionalities and braved her fury. The love now changed into coldness and dislike. It was not merely her woman's impatience of the absurd that made her despise him in her heart, or that prompted the sarcasm in which that contempt found utterance later on. In order to understand her daring mockery, and the cold anger of David's rejoinder, we must read them in the light of the years that had passed. It is probable that Michal had been happy with Paltiel, to whom she had been married on David's banishment.[21]

Let us go back to where King David was in jubilation and celebrating the returned ark of covenant with a 'strange dancing steps.'

2Samuel 6:16

> **And as the ark of the Lord came into the city of David, Michal Saul's daughter looked through a window, and saw King David *LEAPING* and *DANCING* before the LORD; and she *DESPISED* him in her hearth.**

The question comes again, why this sudden hatred for a man she was so much in love with, a man she refused to betrayed to her own father. If not for anything, I guess now should have been the time for Michal to be more happy for David, not only did he come back victorious but become a King of a whole country. Why despising him instead? Because of this act of disloyal to her husband, Michal did pay hugely. How? Definitely not by been barren, it could be " . . . as David's refusal to give her the child which she might wish to have."[22]

Wives must learn to be submissive and love their husbands while on the other hands husbands must love and relate with their wives with respect. (Eph. 5:21-33). A nagging and rebellious wife is only sending her husband out there among the 'wolves'. Learn to correct in humility and in love. If Michal had not despised her husband, she wouldn't have been in such a mess she found herself.

Chapter Fourteen

Barren Versus Had No Child

"Barrenness in women and infertility in men are evils of this present world of sin and death brought about by Adam's disobedience. Barrenness is not punishment on individuals, but like disease, accidents, famines, floods and earthquakes, just another evil that many have to endure. The promise to Israel, had they kept the covenant made with God at Sinai, makes clear that God can and would intervene and ensure fertility of both people and livestock."

Exodus 23:26 There shall nothing cast their young, nor be barren, in thy land: the number of thy days I will fulfil.

Deuteronomy 7:14 Thou shalt be blessed above all people: there shall not be male or female barren among you, or among your cattle.

Psalms 127:3 Lo, children are an heritage of the Lord: and the fruit of the womb is his reward.

After David came back to his house, all these while he was outside *leaping and dancing* before the Lord God who has just granted him victory and returned back to his city the ark of covenant. David was unaware that his once adoring and amiable wife despised everything he was doing outside.

2Samuel 6:20-23

> **20. Then David returned to bless his household. And Michal the daughter of Saul came to meet David and said, How glorious the King of Israel today, who uncovered himself to day, in the eyes of the handmaids of his servants, as one of the vain fellows shamelessly uncovereth himself!**

> **21. And David said to Michal, it was before the Lord, which chose me before thy father and before all his house, to appoint me ruler over the people of the Lord, over Israel; will I play before the Lord.**

> **22. And I will yet be more vile than thus, and will be base in mine own sight: *and of the maidservants which thou has spoken of, of them shall I be had in honour.***

> **23. Therefore Michal the daughter of Saul *had no child* unto the day of her death.**

When you read 2 Samuel Chapter 6:20 closely, you will discover that at the end of Michal's statement, there is an exclamation mark! Exclamation mark after a sentence always depict a sudden surprise or of disgust. The writer could not just but noticed such disgusting words which Michal—a once lover of David has to say to welcome him home.

David, oh boy, gave it to Michal the way she deserved, but one thing he did not do was to curse her neither did Bible recorded that Michal was cursed by God that she will remain barren for life. How could we now conclude that just because Michal despised David and called him names, God is now so angry that He shut the womb of Michal? If that is the case, any woman married to a man of God or a devoted man in the church is in danger of having her womb shut if and when rude or despise her husband. That is never God of the Bible.

To get answer to all these, let us examine the difference between the two words **Barrenness and Had no child** as recorded in the Bible.

WHAT IS BARRENESS?

Barrenness is a term used of a woman or female animals, which are not able to produce children or young.

From the above definition, we will understand that this is in direct contrast to the purpose and commandment to mankind to be fruitful, multiply, produce their kind and replenish the earth. To be barren is the same term used today of medical science—infertility

Modern science divides infertility into two namely:

PRIMARY INFERTILITY: This happens when a woman/man has never experienced conception before after several attempts, usually one year.

SECONDARY INFERTILITY: This described a woman/man that has indeed experience conception once or twice but all of a sudden could not conceive again when she wants to. *(For more information on Infertility, causes and treatment, please consult your Doctor.)*

Both types of infertility are not in the plan of God for man. His plan is that man brings forth his kind. He is the same God when He first gave this commandment as He is today.

The Hebrew word for barren חיצז, (akar) feminine (akarah) denotes probably "uprooted", in the sense of being torn away from the family stock, **and left to wither without progeny or successor.**

Could it be that Michal was left 'to wither without progeny or successor and not necessarily was barren? We shall examine that in the next chapter.

HAD NO CHILD

The word 'had no child' literally means no child. The reason for 'had no child' was given just that she 'had no child'.

2 Samuel 6:23

Therefore Michal the daughter of Saul HAD NO CHILD ... (until the day of her death)

וּלְמִיכַל בַּת־שָׁאוּל לֹא־הָיָה לָהּ יָלֶד עַד יוֹם מוֹתָהּ: פ

Why is it that the Bible does not say "Therefore, Michal the daughter of Saul WAS BARREN . . . . ?"

The original Hebrew word for 'had no child' is דלי אל רבכ which has no meaning and bearing with חיצז translated barren. Let us examine other authorised translations:

2Samuel 6:23

"**Michal the daughter of Saul HAD NO CHILD to the day of her death**" (NASB)

"**And Michal daughter of Saul HAD NO CHILDREN to the day of her death.**" (NIV)

All other Bible translators wrote "HAD NO CHILD", why not 'BARREN'? Let us examined what the bible says about the first woman that was called barren.

Genesis 11:30

But Sarai was BARREN; she had no child. KJV

Sarai was BARREN; she had no child. NASB

Now Sarai was BARREN; she had no children.

וַתְּהִי שָׂרַי עֲקָרָה אֵין לָהּ וָלָד: (Westminster Leningrad Codex)

Why was BARREN used before HAD NO CHILD? Because, Abram and Sarai has been indeed trying to conceive for more than one year without success.

Genesis 16:1-4

1. Now Sarai Abram's wife bare him no children; and she had a handmaid, an Egyptian, whose name was Hagar.

2. And Sarai said unto Abram, Behold now, *the LORD hath restrained me from bearing*: I pray thee, go in unto my maid; it may be that I may obtain children by her. And Abram hearkened to the voice of Sarai.

3. And Sarai Abram's wife took Hagar her maid the Egyptian, *after Abram had dwelt ten years in the land of Canaan,* and gave her to her husband Abram to be his wife.

4. **And he went in unto Hagar, and she conceived: and when she saw that she had conceived, her mistress was despised in her eyes.**

Sarai said to Abram " . . . the Lord hath restrained me from bearing . . ." vs.2 after dwelling in the land of Canaan for ten years. She was called barren this time because she and Abram has been trying to conceive without result (remember our definition of barren). But note that as soon as Abram 'went' in unto Hagar, Sarai's handmaid, she became pregnant!

For what reason(s) God decided to "restrained" Sarai from "bearing" is another topic entirely, but what we do know and that is very certain is that Sarai (later called Sarah) conceived and gave birth to children for Abram (later called Abraham).

Genesis 21:1-3

1. **And the LORD visited Sarah as he had said, and the Lord did unto Sarah as he had spoken.**

2. **For Sarah conceived, *and bare Abraham a son in his old age,* at the set time of which God had spoken to him.**

3. **And Abraham called the name of his son that was born unto him, whom Sarah (not Hagar) bare to him, Isaac.**

Now, let us examine 2 Samuel 6:23 with Genesis 11:30

Genesis 11:30

BUT Sarai was barren; she had no child. (KJV)

2 Samuel 6:23

THEREFORE Micahl the daughter of Saul had no child. (KJV)

The first Chapter, Gen. 11:30 was introduced with **but**. The use of 'but' in a sentence is to introduce a word or phrase that *contrasts* with what was said before (on the contrary). What is that contrast Word?

Genesis 1:27-28

> **27. So God created man in his own image, in the image of God created he him; male and female created he them.**
>
> **28. And God bless them, and God said unto them, Be fruitful, and multiply, and replenish the earth, and subdue it: and have dominion over the fish of the sea, and over the fowl of the air, and over every living thing that moved upon the earth.**

God had commanded man to be fruitful and multiply, yet at old age Sarai has not been able to fulfil that commandment hence the use of "but Sarai was barren . . . ." meaning that Sara condition as at that time was in contrary to what God had earlier promised and commanded—fruitfulness.

The book of 2 Samuel 6:23, starts with **therefore**. When an adverb is used before a sentence, it is telling us a reason for the remaining sentence (for that reason or cause). Look at it this way; 'Therefore' means for that reason—then we can make 2 Samuel 6:23 read like this:

"FOR THAT REASON, Michal the daughter of Saul had no child until the day of her death."

WHAT REASON? Now if we can understand "FOR WHAT REASON" Michal the daughter of Saul had no child, we are not far away from the truth. Let us go back to verse 17 and 21 of 2 Samuel Chapter 6. Michal did not only despise David in her heart she verbally insulted him. If you were in David position, what would you have done? My guess is that most men if in position to do so will simply avoid such a woman who is posing a threat to them. (In David's time' it was allowed to marry more than one woman.) Now, can you remember David's response to Michal?

2Samuel 6:21-22

21. And David said unto Michal, It was before the LORD, which chose me before thy father, and before all his house, to appoint me ruler over the people of the LORD, over Israel: therefore will I play before the LORD.

22. And I will yet be more vile than thus, and will be base in mine own sight: *and of the maidservants which thou hast spoken of, of them shall I be had in honour.*

Could David be saying according to verse 22 in the above statement to Michal that 'since you despise me so much and think I have behaved unruly in the presence of these young ladies, I can as well go with these ladies and leave you alone?' Dr. Constable wrote in his Notes on 2 Samuel thus:

"It may be that God shut Michal's womb as a judgment on her for her attitude (v. 20). One writer believed God judged her for her negative attitude toward the ark. Others have felt that she did not respect her husband or the Lord. Perhaps all these opinions are true. **I think it is more probable, in view of the record of antagonism that precedes verse 23, that we should infer that David had no more intimate relations with her. He had other wives and concubines, and he**

could have fulfilled his sexual desires without Michal. If this interpretation is correct, we have here another instance of David failing God in his family relations. He should have taken the initiative to heal the breach in his relations with Michal that this chapter records and not to have allowed them to continue. Even when we are right, as David was, we must be sensitive to the feelings of those who are wrong, as Michal was, and seek to resolve interpersonal conflicts."[23]

The only punishment David gives to Michal as we shall examine in the next chapter was to avoid her. Michal was not in any way cursed either by David or God. Where these assumptions then come from that Michal was barren as a punishment for her sin. What sin?

Is there any spiritualist, palm readers or fake prophets that has said to you in the time past that your inability to conceive is as a result of your past sin? I have good news for you, once you denounce your sins and genuinely repented and confess Jesus as your Lord and Saviour; your past sins are automatically forgotten and forgiven and cannot be used against your becoming a parent. "I, even I, am he who takes away your sins; and I will no longer keep your evil doings in mind". Isaiah 43:25. [Bible Basic English. BBE]

Chapter Fifteen

Left To Wither Away

"Remember to be gentle with yourself and others. We are all children of chance and none can say why some fields will blossom while others lay brown beneath the August sun. Care for those around you. Look past your differences. Their dreams are no less than yours, their choices no more easily made. And give, give in any way you can, of whatever you possess. To give is to love. To withhold is to wither. Care less for your harvest than for how it is shared and your life will have meaning and your heart will have peace." Kent Nerburn.

In the previous chapter, we discussed barrenness according to Hebrew word-(akar) feminine (akarah) denotes probably "uprooted", in the sense of being torn away from the family stock, and left to wither without progeny or successors.

It is a common practice among the ancient Kings to display their power and authority over their Queens. Some of these Kings does not want a public appearance with their Queens, except for a show of power and splendour.

We have an example of such King in the book of Esther, King Ahasuerus. Ahasuerus was not the name of this particular King, but a title of Persian Kings meaning 'the mighty or venerable King'. (Esther 1:1-2)

This mighty and fearful king never would want any of his queens come or be seen around the palace except been sent for. Violation of this simple but powerful law leads to immediate execution of the offending queen except his 'venerable highness' raises his sceptre in acceptance to see the offending queen. What a king! (Esther 4:11).

On one eventful day, this 'venerable' king had his entire royal guest from other nations, with his own chiefs gathered in his palace for display of royal wealth. After several days of drinking, king Ahasuerus and his guest became intoxicated with wine and thought it wise to parade or make an open show of his beautiful Queen—Vashti in the presence of his drunken guests. (Esther 1:10-11).

The queen who had more sense of moral decency, turn down the king's request not minding the consequences. Most of our ladies should learn a great deal of lesson from this. Some ladies will be willing not only to parade themselves but dance nude in the presence of the guests as far as there is a promised reward! David E. Pratte wrote:

"We may wonder at the wisdom or folly of Vashti's decision. Most commentators uphold her (especially Clarke, Keil, and Zerr). However, some question her conduct (see Henry). Whether she was justified in her refusal or not depends on exactly what the king asked her to do and what her reasons were for refusing, and this seems hard to determine. Obviously the men at the feast were drinking and probably some were drunk. **No self-respecting woman, especially if beautiful and yet modest,**

would want to be a toy displayed before such men. Doubtless she would be submitted to suggestive thoughts and probably even suggestive remarks. Furthermore, Oriental women were generally extremely modest, covering themselves thoroughly, especially in the presence of men. For the men to look on her beauty would require some display. She may have felt this was a violation of her dignity and/or her modesty."[24]

King Ahasuerus felt embarrassed by the action of his queen especially in the presence of his invited guests and chiefs who held him in high esteem. To save the face of the king and prevent further occurrence by other women either in the palace or elsewhere, a royal decree was immediately written:

Esther 1:19

> **If it please the king, let there be a royal commandment from him (Ahasuerus) and let it be written among the laws of Persian and Medes, that it be not altered,** *That Vashti come no more before the king Ahasuerus; and let the king give her royal estate unto another that is better than she.*

The commandment was not to kill queen Vashti, but to demote her from her royal position and much worst, never to have anything-whatsoever-to do with the king; I believe that will include sexual relations. She was to remain in palace but in solitary. Her maidservants will attend to her needs until the day of her death!

Now, the point here is this: if as at the time queen Vashti was 'locked' up for eternity in her own palace for disobeying the king she was yet to have children (the Bible never recorded she had any children though) and the king will never have a sexual relations with her for the rest of her life, will it be right to conclude with the story of Vashti as "Therefore, Vashti, the Queen is BARREN to the day of her death?" Or wont it be better to say "Therefore, Vashti, the Queen HAD NO CHILDREN to the day of her death!"

Think. In that case, Michal was not barren by not been able to conceive (through sexual relation) but had no child because she was simply 'left to wither' (without any man having sexual relations with her) as a punishment for despised her husband, the king of Israel, same way Vashti was left to wither away.

Another incident that confirms that no woman is ever created to be barren except *been torn away from the family stock, and left to wither without progeny or successors* was the incident that involves King David again, though with another women and his son Absalom.

2Samuel 16:20-22

> **20. Then said Absalom to Ahithopel, Give counsel among you what we shall do.**
>
> **21. And Ahithopel said unto Absalom, Go in unto thy father's concubine, which he has left to keep the house; and all Israel shall hear that thou art abhorred of thy father: then shall the hands of all that are with thee be strong.**
>
> **22. So they spread Absalom a tent upon the top of the house; and Absalom went in unto his father's concubines in the sight of all Israel.**

There was a coup d'état in the palace of King David in which he was overthrown by his own son. After the coup, Absalom was advised to sleep i.e. has sexual relations with his father's concubine which he did!

After many battles, David eventually got his palace back and what happened to the defiled concubines? They were locked up in solitary. "And David came to his house at Jerusalem; and the king took the ten women *his* concubines, whom he had left to keep the house, and put them in ward, and fed them, but went not in unto them. So they were shut up unto the day of their death, living in widowhood." 2Sam. 20:3. Every woman must note here and think, if you are not married to that man, you are just a mere 'concubine' and have no respect before men and God.

Now, it will be very illogical to conclude that because the writer says " . . . So they were shut up unto the day of their death, *living in widowhood*" to mean David was dead!

The same will be logical to conclude that these concubines will ' . . . HAD NO CHILDREN, unto the day of their death' which again does not necessarily mean they were barren. They were just 'left to wither away.'

If Michal was a progeny of Adam, who God gave the commandment to be fruitful and replenish the earth to, then it will be wrong and unscriptural to assume or insinuate that the same God will be responsible and made Michal BARREN thereby contradicting Himself. God forbid.

Conclusion

"God is not a man, to say what is false; or the son of man, that his purpose may be changed: what he has said, will he not do? and will he not give effect to the words of his mouth?" NUMBERS 23:19 {BBE}

"For Jesus Christ the Son of God—He who was proclaimed among you by us, that is by Silas and Timothy and myself—did not show Himself a waverer between "Yes" and "No." But it was and always is "Yes" with Him. For all the promises of God, whatever their number, have their confirmation in Him; and for this reason through Him also our "Amen" acknowledges their truth and promotes the glory of God through our faith." 2 Corinthians 1:19-20 [WEYMOUTH].

"Earth and sky will pass away, but it is certain that my words will not pass away." Matthew 24:35. [WEYMOUTH]

Our God is not a man to change His mind at random or provoked into taking irrational steps, His word are "Yes and Amen". If any woman or man is found today childless the fault is never from God, those couple should examine their lives and retraced their steps to the live they lived in the past or living presently.

There could not have been any sin more insulting than which Adam and Eve committed while in the Garden of Eden, a direct defiant and disobedient to their Creator who nurtured them with whatever they wanted. Yet God in His infinity Mercy did not closed the womb of Eve, but rather as a correction and to learn to always trust and obey Him, she is to conceive in pain.

David was indeed a man after God's heart, but he was not without his own shortcomings. He was an adulterer and a murderer, yet God chose to forgive him these sins. To think because Michal despised her husband thereby God in anger or in defence of David shut up her womb for ever is calling God a wicked God. That could possibly infers that any man of God been ridiculed by their spouse is in danger of not having children again!

Whether primary or secondary infertility the root causes can only be traced and find in human themselves. There are many possible causes of infertility. A single cause may not be linked to either the man or the woman. Often the problem stems from a combination of factors in either or both partners. You and your partner will be diagnosed as a couple to determine the best treatment for you.

Infertility in the Man

A man may be infertile because he does not have enough sperm; because the sperm are not active enough; because the passage, or vas deferens, is blocked; or because of problems with ejaculation.

A number of factors can cause or contribute to male infertility:

* Sexually transmitted diseases, such as gonorrhoea or chlamydia, or syphilis.

* Fevers and infections, such as mumps occurring after puberty

* Surgery of the reproductive tract, such as that for undescended testes, hernia repair, disorders of the prostate gland, or cancer.

* Damage to the vas deferens, most often by vasectomy.

* Varicose veins in the scrotum (varicocele).

* Use of certain drugs, such as those for depression or high blood pressure.

* Exposure of the testes to high temperatures, such as those that result from the wearing of tight, unventilated clothing; excessive use of hot tubs; or conditions in the workplace.

* Use of tobacco, marijuana, or alcohol.

* Medical conditions, such as diabetes.

* Genetic or hormonal problems.

* Injury to the testes, such as that resulting from physical trauma or exposure to radiation, can also cause infertility in the man.

Infertility in the Woman

A woman may be infertile because of hormone imbalances or problems in the reproductive tract.

Factors that can cause or add to female infertility include:

* Hormone levels that prevent the release of an egg from an ovary or the implantation of a fertilized egg in the lining of the uterus

* Extra weight (more than 30% over her ideal body weight), which may cause problems with ovulation.

* Scarring or tumours of the uterus or defects of the uterus present from birth.

* Too little or poor-quality cervical mucus, sometimes due to surgery or other treatment.

* Endometriosis—a condition in which tissue like that normally lining the uterus (the endometrium) is found outside the uterus.

* Adhesions-bands of scar tissue from previous surgery, endometriosis, or infections that bind together tissues inside the abdomen.

* Infections such as pelvic inflammatory disease (PID), a severe infection of the female reproductive organs that may be caused by sexually transmitted diseases such as gonorrhoea or chlamydia; or appendicitis, which can result in scarring of the internal pelvic organs.

* Production of antibodies that attack her partner's sperm.

* Medical conditions, such as thyroid disease or diabetes.

* Genetic conditions such as Turner's syndrome, in which a woman has only one X chromosome and may not completely develop breasts or pubic hair.

* Use of tobacco, marijuana, or alcohol.[25]

With all the aforementioned conditions, there is none of them that are caused by God.

Perhaps you have been waiting too long for the fruit of wombs, seek medical and expertise opinion on the root cause of your barrenness, take and adhere to all suggestions, treatment and advice given. Above all, have absolute faith in God that He alone can give you the fruit of the womb and nobody else.

He that created you has the spare parts of your body. It doesn't matter what damages might have been done to your womb or sperms, if you cry unto Him and believe in Him – He will surely restore everything back to normal for the promise of God is "NONE SHALL BE BARREN".

SOLUTION PRAYER POINTS ON BARRENNESS

- Let all spiritual parasites that are feeding on the seeds of my womb be roasted in the name of Jesus.

- Lord, correct any disorder in the functioning of my ovary, fallopian tube and womb supernaturally in the name of Jesus.

- Let all fire and thunder of God destroy any demonic padlock used by the enemy to lock my womb in the name of Jesus.

- Lord, activate my womb for conception in the name of Jesus.

- Every vicious cycle of problems in my life should break in the name of Jesus.

- No devourer will devour the fruit of my womb in the name of Jesus.

- I soak my womb, fallopian tube and ovary with the blood of Jesus.

- I claim the promises of God concerning child bearing in the name of Jesus.

- I decree the exit of all spiritual poison that entered into my womb during my wedding ceremony in Jesus name.

- Spiritual poison introduced into my womb through eating in the dream I command you to depart completely in Jesus name.

- Spiritual poison introduced into my womb through sexual intercourse in the dream I command you to depart completely in Jesus name.

- Lord, I desire breakthroughs concerning—childbearing today in the name of Jesus.

- Lord, I desire breakthroughs concerning pregnancy this month in the name of Jesus.

- Lord I desire breakthroughs concerning delivery of my baby this year in the name of Jesus.

- Fire of God, saturate my womb now, in Jesus name.

- I dismiss and disband from my heart every thought, image of picture of failure in the matter of conception in Jesus name.

- I reject every curse of miscarriage and pre—mature birth in my family.

- I declare that there shall be no barrenness in my life.

- Every destructive that has entered into my reproductive organs be removed by fire.

- I break any curse contrary to childbearing transferred to me by any boyfriend/girlfriend.

- I arrest every hormonal/problem in the name of Jesus.

- Let the walls of my womb be purged by divine fire.

- I cast out every spirit of death from my womb.

- Spiritual poison introduced into my womb through demonic contamination I command you to depart completely in the name of Jesus.

- Spiritual poison introduced into my womb through spiritual incision I command you to depart completely in Jesus name.

- Spiritual poison introduced into my womb through abortion I command you to depart completely in the name of Jesus.

- Spiritual poison introduced into my womb through masturbation I command you to depart completely in Jesus name.

- Spiritual poison introduced into my womb through demonic sexual partner I command you to depart completely in the name of Jesus.

- Spiritual poison introduced into my womb through remote control mechanism I command you to depart completely in the name of Jesus.

Bibliography

Boulay, R.A. Flying Serpents and Dragons: The story of Mankind's Reptilian Past. Escondilo, California: The book Tree; 1999.

Morris, M. The Genesis Record. California,U.S.A: Baker Book House; 1976.

Dixon, J. Genesis Expository Thoughts. Darlington,U.S.A: Evangelical Press; 2005.

Wenham, J. Genesis 1-15, Word Biblical Commentary, Waco: Word books;1987.

Elizabeth Wayne Mark: The covenant of circumcision: mew perspectives on an ancient Jewish rite

Young, J. Genesis 3 A devotional and expository study, Edinburgh: TBTT;1983.

Hamilton, P. Handbook on The Pentateuch. U.S.A: Baker Books; 1999.

Davidson, R.Genesis 1-11: Cambridge: Cambridge University press; 1973.

Rick, W. The purpose Driven Life, USA: Zondervan; 2002.

Myles, M. Understanding your Potentials, Destiny Image publishers; 1992.

Rao, DK & Kaur, JJ. Biology 10. Ratna Sagar publisher; 2009.

Sebastian, K. Ministers and ministries in the local church: a comprehensive guide to ecclesiastical norms: St Pauls BYB, publishing; 2005.

Arriola, E. Celebrating Life with God, Rex Bookstore, Inc. publishing.

James, B. Law, Sex, and Christian Society in Medieval Europe, University of Chicago press; 1990.

Donald, P., The Conjugal Act as Personal Act: A Study of the Catholic Concept of the Conjugal Act in the Light of Christian Anthropology, Ignatius Press; 2002.

Alexander, Rosner, T. S. eds. New dictionary of Biblical Theology. England: Intervasity Press;2000.

Dennery, B. Covenant Key to the Scripture. USA: 2009.

Constable, L., Notes on 2 Samuel. http://www.soniclight.com/constable/notes/pdf/2samuel.pdf

ENDNOTES

[1]1 John SH Tay God's Destiny for You

[2] Boulay, R.A. Flying Serpents and Dragons: The story of Mankind's Reptilian Past. Escondilo,California: The book Tree; 1999. Pg. 85

[3] Morris, M. The Genesis Record. California,U.S.A: Baker Book House; 1976. Pg.112

[4] Dixon, J. Genesis Expository Thoughts. Darlington,U.S.A: Evangelical Press; 2005. Pg.70

[5] Wenham, J. Genesis 1-15, Word Biblical commentary, Waco: word books;1987. P72

[6] Young, J. Genesis 3 A devotional and expository study. Edinburgh: TBTT;1983.pg.17

[7] Dixon, J. Genesis Expository Thoughts. Darlington,U.S.A: Evangelical Press; 2005. Pg. 80.

[8] Hamilton, P. Handbook on The Pentateuch. U.S.A: Baker Books; 1999. Pg. 49

[9] Rick, W. the purpose Driven Life. USA: Zondervan; 2002.

[10] Myles, M. Understanding your potentials. Destiny Image publishers; 1992. Pg 146

[11] Culled from the journal: Patient.co.uk

[12] Culled from webMD journal www.webmd.com

[13] Rao, DK & Kaur, JJ. Biology 10. Ratna Sagar publisher; 2009. Pg 132

[14] Sebastian, K. Ministers and ministries in the local church: a comprehensive guide to ecclesiastical norms: St Pauls BYB, publishing; 2005. Pg 382

[15] Arriola, E. Life with God/Celebrating Life with God 5-tm Rev. Rex Bookstore, Inc. publishing. Pg 94

[16] James, B. Law, sex, and Christian society in medieval Europe. University of Chicago press; 1990. Pg 57

[17] Donald, P. the conjugal act as personal act: a study of the catholic concept of the conjugal ct in the light of Christian anthropology. Ignatius Press; 2002. Pg 4-6

[18] Alexander, Rosner, T. S. eds. New dictionary of Biblical Theology. England: Intervasity Press;2000. Pg 420

[19] Dennery, B. Covenant key to the Scripture. USA: 2009. Pg 86

[20] Elizabeth Wayne Mark: The covenant of circumcision: mew perspectives on an ancient Jewish rite

[21] David J. A. Clines and Tamara Cohn Eskenazi: Telling Queen Michal's story: an experiment in comparative interpretation.

[22] Peter R. Ackroyd: The second book of Samuel: commentary.

[23] L. Constable, Notes on 2 Samuel. http://www.soniclight.com/constable/notes/pdf/2samuel.pdf

[24] Culled from the journal gospel way.

[25] Culled from Home Fertility Network Journal.

24031227R00065

Printed in Great Britain
by Amazon